Rave reviews from leading marriage experts, pastors, and counselo

Getting Ready for Mar

"Most of us spend more time preparing for our vocations than we do preparing for ... be that is why we are more successful in our jobs than in our marriages. Yet life's meaning is not found in money but in relationships, and marriage is designed to be the most intimate human relationship. If you want a successful marriage, then spend time preparing. *Getting Ready for Marriage* is an excellent and practical tool to aid you in the process. I highly recommend it."

Gary Chapman, PhD, author of *The 5 Love Languages*

"Before you say 'I do,' read this book! Jim and Doug have directed scores of people in the direction of healthy, happy, vibrant marriages. They can do the same for you."

Max Lucado, pastor and *New York Times* bestselling author

"*Getting Ready for Marriage* is filled with practical, biblical insights gleaned from Jim Burns' and Doug Fields' years of experience counseling couples. I wish every engaged couple could read through this book together before tying the knot!"

Jim Daly, president of Focus on the Family

"I absolutely love this book! Over years of research with singles and those dating and married, I've seen a need for a simple, compelling book like this, one that will walk a couple through the process of ... well ... getting ready for marriage! I'm thrilled Jim and Doug have put this together. Everyone contemplating marriage, and everyone helping couples who want to get married, will want this outstanding resource!"

Shaunti Feldhahn, social researcher and bestselling
author of *For Women Only* and *For Men Only*

"I've never known which book to recommend to engaged couples—until now. Jim and Doug have taken their combined seventy years of marital wisdom and boiled it down to the pressing questions and practical ideas every couple needs to read."

Kara Powell, PhD, executive director of Fuller Youth Institute

"Marriage is one of God's greatest gifts. But to be fully experienced, it requires some peeks under the hood before driving it off the lot. This makes the probability of lifetime love, intimacy, and friendship much more of a reality. Jim Burns and Doug Fields have written an essential book for the premarital relationship. Highly recommended."

Dr. John Townsend, author of the bestselling Boundaries
series, psychologist, and leadership consultant

"We all hear that marriage is hard work and that we need to be prepared. Now Jim Burns and Doug Fields have written a book to do just that—prepare people for marriage. In their honest and witty style, they offer practical help that can guide couples as they prepare for the greatest adventure of all. I highly recommend this book and think it would make a great wedding gift!"

Holly Wagner, pastor of Oasis Church and founder of GodChicks

"As a pastor, I'm so excited for fresh material to help couples prepare for marriage. This is a much-needed resource! I know this content is excellent because I've seen it help young couples in our very own church—both Doug and Jim are leaders at Mariners and are committed to helping our marriages succeed. I'm so excited to have them share what they're doing here with others around the world."

Kenton Beshore, senior pastor of Mariners Church

"With about one-third of Christian marriages ending in divorce, about one-third in misery, and another one-third ranging from doing okay to great, we obviously need this book. Both Jim and Doug have shown in their personal and professional lives that they know what they are talking about. I hope a lot of churches make this required reading before marriage in their church."

Steve Arterburn, president of New Life Ministries
and *New York Times* bestselling author

"As I read through this outstanding book, I kept thinking, *I wish Kay and I had this resource before we were married.* Far too many of the 2.4 million couples who get married each year are not adequately prepared to make it work. I am so happy that there's a book like this where every page is filled with practical God-honoring advice."

Rick Warren, pastor and author of *The Purpose Driven Life*

JIM BURNS & DOUG FIELDS

GETTING READY FOR MARRIAGE

WORKBOOK

David C Cook
transforming lives together

GETTING READY FOR MARRIAGE WORKBOOK
Published by David C Cook
4050 Lee Vance View
Colorado Springs, CO 80918 U.S.A.

David C Cook Distribution Canada
55 Woodslee Avenue, Paris, Ontario, Canada N3L 3E5

David C Cook U.K., Kingsway Communications
Eastbourne, East Sussex BN23 6NT, England

The graphic circle C logo is a registered trademark of David C Cook.

ISBN 978-0-7814-1218-6
eISBN 978-0-7814-1284-1

© 2015 Jim Burns, Doug Fields
The Author is represented by and this book is published in association with the literary
agency of WordServe Literary Group, Ltd., www.wordserveliterary.com.

The Team: Ingrid Beck, Gwen Ellis, Amy Konyndyk, Carly Razo, Helen Macdonald, Karen Athen
Interior Design: Rodney Bissell
Cover Design: Nick Lee
Cover Photo: Shutterstock

Printed in the United States of America
First Edition 2015

3 4 5 6 7 8 9 10 11 12

091415

CONTENTS

CONGRATULATIONS!

We are excited for you and your upcoming journey. You are entering into something that many fear, some mock, others delight in, and nearly everyone attempts: marriage. It's a big deal … a *really* big deal.

> If you are seriously dating but not yet engaged or want to find out if you should move toward engagement, this workbook is also for you. Simply replace the word "fiancé" with the name of the person you're dating, and bingo, this workbook is now for you too.

You are wise to recognize the importance of preparing for one of the most significant decisions of your life. We want to help you do more than make a committed attempt at success; after completing this workbook, we want you to be prepared to develop, and thrive in, an exceptionally beautiful marriage. We are big fans of marriage and believe it's the most exciting and transforming relationship in the entire world.

But!

We've also been married long enough (seventy years combined between our two marriages) to know that it isn't easy. In our book *Getting Ready for Marriage*, we ask couples if they would willingly board a plane if they knew it had a 30 to 50 percent chance of crashing. Seems crazy, right? No one in their right mind would take that risk.

But did you know those are the same percentages of failed marriages? Too many couples are willing to embark on the marriage journey without intentional preparation to avoid disaster. That's why we've taken concepts from our book and put them into exercises for this workbook.

We're definitely not anticipating disaster for you, but we know you will experience some relational turbulence as a couple—every married couple does! That's why spending time thinking through and talking about the issues in this workbook is so important to the future health of your marriage. Anyone can plan a wedding, but it's the wise couple that prepares for a marriage. You are taking wise steps, and we're excited to help you on your journey.

For those reading a book like this or involved with premarital counseling, the chance of divorce decreases by 31 percent.[1] Please pause to think deeply about that statistic for a moment …

HOW TO USE THIS BOOK

There's no one right way to use this workbook. **You may approach the material in whatever way works best for you. It really is that flexible! We have designed the exercises on the following pages to help you think and communicate about important issues while honestly expressing your expectations to each other. Within this flexibility we have some suggestions to help you get the most out of your experience.**

Each of you should have your own workbook.

Our companion book, *Getting Ready for Marriage*, is one you can share and read together, but this workbook is intended for you to complete as an individual. Having your own will allow you to work on the exercises whenever you have a few moments rather than waiting until you are with your fiancé.

Fight the temptation to save a few dollars by sharing the workbook—it will add **so much more value if you each have your own copy**. (If money is an issue, don't be afraid to ask for help. Probably someone in your life would gladly buy you a second workbook, knowing it will ultimately help your future marriage.)

We guarantee you will get much more out of this experience if you complete these exercises on your own—reflecting deeply on yourself and your relationship—and then share your answers as a couple.

Schedule a weekly time to talk about your answers.

We advise couples to set aside about an hour each week to discuss the exercises they've completed. If you're in a long-distance relationship, you'll want to be even more intentional to create time within your schedule to make this happen. Maybe you think that talking about your upcoming marriage won't be as fun as planning your wedding. However, we believe that if you choose to, you can have a great time in these discussions. You will get to know your fiancé in new ways, understanding who he or she is and what is within his or her heart possibly better than you ever have. And we think that's pretty exciting.

Take your workbook to premarital or mentoring sessions.

After you've shared your answers with your fiancé and discussed the provided questions, we encourage you to share your results, issues, and major conversation points with whoever (a counselor, pastor, or marriage mentor) is guiding you through the premarital process.

If you are not participating in premarital counseling or don't have anyone walking you through this process, find someone. Look around at couples you admire, and ask one to mentor you throughout your engagement. If the couple has never done this sort of thing before, our book *Getting Ready for Marriage* has some helpful advice to guide them as mentors.

Choose the exercises that trigger your interest.

There are three exercises in each chapter. Ideally, we want you to go through all of the exercises in the workbook. If you can do this, it would be best to complete them in the order in which they're written. However, if time is an issue and you're forced to be selective, choose at least one exercise from each chapter to work through. Whether it is a shorter one that requires less time or a longer one that encourages more reflection, each exercise will prompt significant discussion.

We're consistently stunned by how many engaged couples are so focused on planning their single-day wedding celebration that they put relatively little energy into planning their married future. Don't make that mistake!

Make a plan for how to use your time together.

We've learned from working with many couples that the best results are achieved by those who set specific times and deadlines to work through this material.

For example, make it a goal to finish all the exercises in a chapter on your own over the course of one week. Then, meet with your fiancé for an hour during the weekend to discuss your answers.

Obviously, this is dependent on how much time you have before the wedding. But we strongly believe that the more conversation and honest connection you have prior to marriage, the better your marriage will be.

> **Don't underestimate the power of a healthy conversation. It can form the pathway that will guide you away from future pain.**

At the end of each exercise, we encourage you to write down anything you would like to talk about with your fiancé and/or a marriage counselor.

One Final Thought

If you find that the thoughts and discussions triggered as you work through this book bring up red flags in your relationship, **please don't be afraid to slow everything down**. Get some help—there is just too much at stake not to. Seek the counsel of a marriage mentor, a trusted pastor, or a professional counselor.

More than one-third of all engaged couples don't make it to their wedding day. Many of these couples made courageous decisions that saved them from future divorce or heartbreak. If you are running into major issues in your relationship, one of the best decisions you can make is to take more time during the engagement process to work through these concerns. We have never met a couple who regretted slowing things down to work on red flags and roadblocks.

If you make a decision to delay your wedding, don't worry what others will think. Other people are not responsible for your future marriage—you are. You and your fiancé will have to navigate the pressures and pain of an unprepared marriage. If you need more time, please—we beg you—take it.

You don't want a marriage built on hope. If needed, it's vital that you be brave enough to delay or cancel your wedding. If you must do so, you won't be the first. Between 35 and 40 percent of all engagements in this country are broken or canceled.

QUESTIONS TO ASK BEFORE YOU CHOOSE A PREMARITAL COUNSELOR OR MENTOR

"Where there is no counsel, the people fall; but in the multitude of counselors there is safety" (Proverbs 11:14 NKJV).

Below are some questions to consider. For more specific ideas on choosing a mentor couple, see the third exercise in chapter 8, found on page 112. Is there a pastor or couple you admire who you would like to have walk alongside you through premarital counseling or marriage mentoring?

"Think about it: you would never have a surgical procedure without seeking the advice of a doctor. Unfortunately, too many couples don't invest the time (or the money) they should to get crucial relational advice and guidance through premarital counseling.

When will you contact this person or couple?

How often would you like to meet with them?

What are your goals and expectations from your time with them?

List some of the specific areas of conversation you want to address with them.

Can this material be used for pre-engagement?

Yes. *Oui. Ja. Si.* In any language, the answer is YES!

Ideally, you spend time discussing these subjects prior to engagement, and then spend your engaged time working on the details of your wedding and enhancing your relationship. It's very wise to begin thinking seriously about marriage and your future *before* you get engaged. Again, anyone can *plan* a wedding, but it takes wisdom to *prepare* for a marriage.

We encourage those who are genuinely considering marriage (pre-engaged) to begin having serious conversations about the issues addressed in this workbook. If more couples would take time during pre-engagement to discuss their history, fears, expectations, dreams, and the rest of the topics in this workbook, more marriages would get off to a better start.

Specific notes to pastors, counselors, and marriage mentors on how to best use this workbook may be found on page 124. And if you are new to marriage mentoring, there is additional information for you there as well.

The Getting Ready for Marriage online tool provides valuable resources to help build stronger communication in your marriage. Visit GettingReadyforMarriage.com for videos, discussion starters, and communication assessment experiences. They are life-changing!

CHAPTER ONE

ARE YOU READY FOR MARRIAGE?

As you move toward marriage, you need to ask the right questions about yourself, your fiancé, and your future—and give deep thought to the answers. Chances are good that you're tired of questions connected to your wedding: flowers, catering, guest list, and so on. "Question fatigue" is understandable and common among those who are engaged.

For your marriage to thrive, your best energy shouldn't be spent planning a wedding party that only lasts a few hours; your best efforts should be given to thinking about your lifelong marriage.

Exercises

☐ **My Story**

☐ **Five Crucial Questions**

☐ **My Baggage**

① EXERCISE ONE

My Story

Take time to reflect and write about your life, your relationship, and your family. Who you are today is the sum total of your experiences, so in order to fully know each other, you and your fiancé should understand how your life experiences as well as your families have shaped each of you. The clearer you are, the more helpful this exercise is. Be sure to share this exercise with your premarital counselor.

> **You are the sum total of your past experiences, and the more you understand about yourself and one another, the easier it will be to become one in your marriage.**

My name:..

My fiancé's name:..

My hobbies and interests:.......................................
....
....
....
....

My highest level of education completed:
....

My current occupation:...

Our Relationship

(As difficult as it might be, reduce the story of your relationship to one paragraph that highlights the key moments or story lines.)

How long we have been dating:

What I like best about my fiancé:

Met he is a hero
Todd: happy

We are opposite in these areas:

-Activity level
— extrovert vs. Introvert

I am most attracted to my fiancé when:

-both said happy/playful
— todd said: ~~not necessary~~ present
— ~~H~~Mel: with Me as a team

The most defining moment in our relationship was:

Ø

One tension we seem to regularly return to is:

Forget about each other

In our time together, my absolute favorite moment was:

— when she Met Me in the rain
— scooters in the Rain

My Family

I would describe my relationship with my mom as _____ (one word), because …

I would describe my relationship with my dad as _____ (one word), because …

Are you closer to your mom or dad? Why?

How have your siblings affected your life in both positive and negative ways?

What did you learn about relationships from your parents and family?

Describe the home environment you grew up in:

What was the emotional temperature of your home (for example: warm and fun, heated and filled with tension, cold and distant)?

How did your parents view money, saving, and spending?

What were some important family traditions?

Describe the spiritual tone within your home:

List any tragic or big events within your family during your growing-up years:

My Significant Moments

Every person has significant markers throughout their life. These might include great accomplishments or painful experiences, but each memory, event, and experience adds to the story of who you are today. List at least two positive and two negative moments for each of the following time periods in your life.

" It's amazing to us that some premarital couples haven't shared their personal histories, expectations, hopes, dreams, or even life goals. Your backstory is essential material that makes up the depth of who you are today. Your fiancé needs to know it all.

Significant moments include ...

Birth–Kindergarten

Elementary Years

Junior High & High School

Post High School–Present

As you talk about these defining moments with your fiancé, listen actively, encourage one another, and be willing to go deeper. Don't be afraid to ask tough follow-up questions such as:

"How do you think that part of your story will impact our future?"

"What would be the most helpful way to tell you when you're beginning to act like your dad or mom? I don't want to dishonor you, but you mentioned that specific attitude that you picked up from your mom could become an issue with us."

Remember, you're going to learn everything about your future spouse eventually; it's better to learn it now and openly discuss it *before* you get married so there aren't as many surprises and issues to work out after marriage.

When we're together (or with our premarital counselor), be sure to talk about:

Date we discussed this exercise:

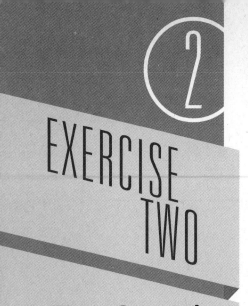

EXERCISE TWO

Five Crucial Questions

Most of our premarital counseling sessions begin with five questions couples need to answer before they say "I do!" These questions are not always easy to answer, but they're definitely essential and worthy of discussion. (Take time to write out or discuss your answers.)

> **Successful marriages are often the product of healthy premarital decisions and a willingness to work on the relationship before saying "I do."**

1. Are you willing to work at premarital education?

What does "work" mean to you in the context of your engagement and premarital counseling?

How much time per week do you plan to commit to premarital preparation, including premarital counseling sessions and reading and discussing this workbook or other materials you may use?

How do you think your fiancé will respond to the question above? Do you feel you are on the same page in regard to premarital education?

2. Are you willing to hear from your relational community?

Who are some significant people in your life you will invite to share observations of your relationship?

What will you ask them?

How will you respond if one of those people expresses concerns?

"It is important to have family and friends who will be honest with you about how they view your relationship. It would be wise for you to give permission to those you trust to speak truth before your wedding day.

3. Are you willing to look honestly at red flags?

Do you currently have concerns with any of the issues below?

Yes	No	Need to discuss
○	⊗	Addiction
○	⊗	Abuse
○	⊗	Unfaithfulness
○	⊗	Friends or family concerns
○	⊗	Cohabitating/living together before marriage
○	⊗	Sexual activity or expectations
○	⊗	Children
○	⊗	Spiritual values
○	○	Communication
○	○	Conflict resolution
○	⊗	Previous spouses
○	○	Interests and ideas about leisure time
○	○	Habits or personality
○	⊗	Finances
○	⊗	Character concerns
○	⊗	Health issues

(handwritten note: "climb more ↓" pointing to "Interests and ideas about leisure time"; circles drawn around Communication, Conflict resolution, Interests and ideas about leisure time, and Habits or personality)

> People who ignore red flags in a relationship—by not talking about their issues, or worse, hoping the issues will simply go away—are headed toward disaster. They often marry, become miserable, and divorce (either quickly or after dragging it out for years). Talk about these things now rather than later.

For more information on why we think these are potential red flags, read pages 34–36 in the *Getting Ready for Marriage* book.

4. Are you willing to be brutally honest about your own brokenness?

What is one personal pain you are bringing into this relationship?

How will you tell your fiancé about past hurts? Do you feel safe enough to share? How do you think he or she will respond?

What can you do to help your fiancé feel safe about sharing his or her past pain?

> You will be ready for marriage not when you have your life in perfect order, but rather when you are willing to admit to yourself, your fiancé, and God that you need healing for your brokenness.

5. Are you ready for unconditional commitment?

What do the words below mean to you?

I, _____, take you,

_____, to be my wife/husband. I

promise before God and these witnesses to be your

loving and faithful husband/wife in plenty and in

want, in sickness and in health, in joy and in sorrow,

in good times and hard times, with God's grace and

strength, as long as we both shall live.

How do you hope your fiancé responds to that same question?

While these five questions may seem unromantic in comparison to discussions about your honeymoon, we believe spending time on this exercise can provide you a sense of confidence and hope. If any of these questions and answers revealed deeper issues, we encourage you to seek wise counsel immediately.

When we're together (or with our premarital counselor), be sure to talk about:

Date we discussed this exercise:

EXERCISE THREE

My Baggage

Every person is a combination of strengths and weaknesses. There will never be a perfect marriage because one imperfect person is marrying another imperfect person. We all bring some sort of relational or emotional baggage into our marriage.

The question to answer isn't, "Will my past (or my baggage) impact my marriage?" That's a given; it will. The better question is, "When my baggage surfaces in marriage, will my spouse be aware of it, and are we prepared to deal with it?"

Most marriage experts say the two most neglected areas of personal communication are sexual and financial history. Don't spring surprises on your spouse in the future when you could talk about these issues before you marry.

What good qualities do you bring into the relationship?

What negative traits do you bring into the relationship?

> **Despite what you've grown up seeing in movies, the success of your marriage is not determined by finding the "right person." Your marital success and happiness depend on you *becoming* the right person.**

How have you been hurt by others in your life? Parents? Friends? Past relationships? Have those hurts created emotional or relational scars you carry with you still? If so, what are they?

What mistakes or regrets do you carry with you from your past?

How do your past hurts and mistakes currently affect your choices, personality, and relationships?

> "Having honest dialogue about the issues you face as an individual and as a couple is crucial to moving your relationship forward. If you think to yourself, *I don't know if I can share that with him or her*, that means you need to.

Does your fiancé know about the baggage you'll be bringing into marriage, and is he or she understanding of it?

Is there anything you are holding back from your past that could impact your relationship?

Make your fiancé feel safe and forgiven; no judgment or condemnation—only understanding. Handled with love, this exercise will bring you closer to one another.

What gives you confidence that you are ready for marriage considering your past hurts and regrets?

In light of these issues, how can your fiancé best love and care for you?

When we're together (or with our premarital counselor), be sure to talk about:

> It is the hidden things that later make marriages sick or sometimes fail. It's only fair that both parties going into a marriage have the full story—no matter how painful it is to tell or hear.

This exercise may lead to some tension and tough conversations, but those discussions will test and prove that you can face difficult times both now and in the future. Be courageous enough to care for your upcoming marriage right now. Talking about the baggage each of you brings into your marriage will not only bring you closer now, but it will also bring healing, hope, and grace to your relationship moving forward.

Date we discussed this exercise:

CHAPTER TWO

WRITING YOUR MARRIAGE SCRIPT THROUGH GOALS, HOPES, AND EXPECTATIONS

You are getting ready to write a story with the most important person in your life. It's going to be an exciting story that you'll continue to write for many more years.

Your personal story has a unique backstory that contributes to who you are today. That story needs to be articulated, and your fiancé needs to know it well, understand it, and embrace it. Hopefully, the exercises in chapter 1 helped you do this.

Your marriage is also going to tell a story, and we know it can be a great one. The exercises in this chapter will help you and your fiancé work together to decide what you want your future story to be as you dream and set goals.

As you share your answers with each other or your marriage mentor, pay special attention to the words you and your fiancé chose to write. Words matter, and specific words may need to be further discussed. Don't be afraid to ask clarifying questions. Good questions lead to great dialogue.

Exercises

☐ My Expectations

☐ Making S.M.A.R.T. Goals

☐ Where I See Hope in Our Relationship

EXERCISE ONE

My Expectations

It's impossible to enter into marriage without expectations; everyone has them, even if they don't know how to verbalize them clearly. Expectations determine how you operate and engage with your spouse, and those same expectations become your default way of thinking about your spouse.

This is your opportunity to think through your expectations and express them gently. Many marriage conflicts come from unspoken or unrealistic expectations. By spending significant time on this now, you will be able to save yourself significant pain later.

Roles and Relationship

How will you make decisions as a couple? Be as specific as possible, considering difficult decisions about such things as buying a home, job changes, children, disciplining children, in-laws, and relocating.

What actions will you take when you disagree on a decision?

How will you handle your calendar and the daily schedule of events and responsibilities?

What roles do you envision being different in your relationship than were observed in your parents' or stepparents' relationships?

> While we appreciate the optimism of the engaged couple who doesn't think they'll have any issues in their marriage, we also agree with Drs. Les and Leslie Parrott, who reveal that "happily married couples will have healthy expectations of marriage."[1]

Finances

How will you manage your budget?

For additional discussion, there are three financial exercises beginning on page 81 of this workbook.

How will major decisions about finances be made?

Choose a number that best describes how you feel about debt. Then circle the number that describes how you think your fiancé feels about debt.

	I don't ever want any debt				A little debt is fine			I'm comfortable with debt		
Me:	1	2	3	4	5	6	7	8	9	10
Fiancé:	1	2	3	4	5	6	7	8	9	10

When you were growing up, how did your parents handle money? Who was in charge of your family finances?

Did money feel tight? Was it important to spend money to have fun? Was spending for pleasure frowned upon?

What will you do differently with your finances when you're married?

Children and Family

Will you have children? If so, how many, and when?

Which style best describes how you plan to parent your children?

Authoritarian: Children are expected to follow clearly established rules. Failure to follow rules results in clear consequences and punishment.

Authoritative: Similar to authoritarian but more democratic. These parents listen to their children's questions and are more forgiving than punishing.

Permissive: Few demands of children, low expectations, more of a friend than a traditional parent.

Describe your future parenting style in more detail.

What style did your parents display, and how do you think that will impact your parenting?

Has someone in your life been a model or mentor in terms of parenting? What have you learned from him or her that you want to bring into your future family?

What would you do if you were unable to conceive?

Do you both plan to have careers? If so, who will be the primary caregiver for your children?

Home

Where do you want to live?

Where does your fiancé want to live?

What if you and your fiancé differ on this answer?

Are there any living locations that are in the "No way I'm ever living there" zone?

When do you anticipate buying a home?

Who do you envision being responsible for the following?

Grocery shopping

Cleaning the house

Taking out the trash

Laundry

Yard work

Where do you see you and your fiancé living in

Five years?

Ten years?

During retirement?

Sex Life

What are you looking forward to in regard to your sexual relationship?

For additional discussion on sex, there are three exercises beginning on page 95 of this workbook.

What fears do you have about your physical relationship?

Sometimes couples have struggles with their sex life. Are you willing to seek counsel in this area? If so, where would you go for help?

Spiritual Life

Choose a number that describes your spiritual expectations and then what you think your fiancé's are.

	No interest		I'll keep my faith to myself		Occasionally pray together			Spiritual intimacy	
Me:	1	2	3	4	5	6	7	8	9	10
Fiancé:	1	2	3	4	5	6	7	8	9	10

What is your philosophy about attending church together?

As a couple, how important is it that you pray together? If it's important, how often? Do you see any obstacles to this?

How will you provide spiritual encouragement to each other?

When we're together (or with our premarital counselor), be sure to talk about:

How would you like to receive spiritual encouragement?

This exercise on expectations should have triggered some lively discussions. It's not wrong to have specific expectations; it only becomes wrong if they're not expressed or they're unrealistic. Don't expect your fiancé to be a mind reader. Speak honestly. Speak truthfully. Speak gently. Speak with the knowledge that you can share your heart with each other and come to a mutual understanding of what each of you expects.

We find this is an excellent exercise to share with a counselor. Those with marriage experience are often helpful at shedding some light on unrealistic expectations. Be willing to drop your pride, humble yourself, and learn. The future of your marriage depends on it.

For additional discussions about your spiritual life, there are three exercises starting on page 105 of this workbook.

Date we discussed this exercise:

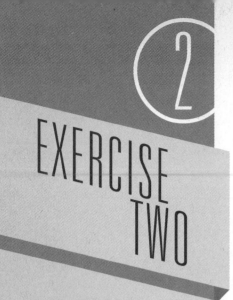

2

EXERCISE TWO

Making S.M.A.R.T. Goals

Many relationships suffer from what has been called "the drift." Couples simply drift from their intended target of a healthy marriage. When this happens, they need to make conscious decisions to correct the drift.

That's where goals come in: they can be a powerful ally for a couple, keeping them aligned or bringing them back together if they begin to drift. Author Zig Ziglar once said, "If you aim at nothing, you will hit it every time." The season of engagement offers couples the perfect opportunity to clarify individual goals as well as shared goals.

To help you with this goal-setting exercise, consider writing goals that are S.M.A.R.T.

SPECIFIC:

Is your goal clear and specifically stated?

MEASURABLE:

Can you quantify or put numbers and measurements to the goal?

ATTAINABLE:

Is the goal realistic, feasible, or even possible given what you want to do and the time in which you're giving yourself?

RELEVANT:

What is the practical impact achieving this goal will have on your life and values?

TIME-BOUND:

When will you reach your goal?

> **When a couple is thoughtful and purposeful with their choices to be in an authentic relationship of oneness, outlining future goals is essential. Goals help couples get where they want to go. They provide direction and give hope for the future.**

In the following exercise, write two short-term goals: one for yourself and one for you as a couple. A short-term goal could be accomplished within a month or before your wedding date. Repeat the same steps for long-term goals. A long-term goal might be one that is at least a year and could last up to several years.

#1 My short-term individual goal is:

What will be the primary benefit of achieving this goal?

SPECIFIC: What exactly will you accomplish?

MEASURABLE: How will you and others know when you have reached your goal?

ATTAINABLE: Is attaining this goal realistic, and do you have the resources and ability to achieve the goal?

RELEVANT: Why is this goal important to you?

TIME-BOUND: When will you achieve this goal?

#2 My long-term individual goal is:

What will be the primary benefit of achieving this goal?

SPECIFIC: What exactly will you accomplish?

MEASURABLE: How will you and others know when you have reached your goal?

ATTAINABLE: Is attaining this goal realistic, and do you have the resources and ability to achieve the goal?

RELEVANT: Why is this goal important to you?

TIME-BOUND: When will you achieve this goal?

#3 A short-term goal for us as a couple is:

What will be the primary benefit of achieving this goal?

SPECIFIC: What exactly will you accomplish?

MEASURABLE: How will you and others know when you have reached your goal?

ATTAINABLE: Is attaining this goal realistic, and do you have the resources and ability to achieve the goal?

RELEVANT: Why is this goal important to you?

TIME-BOUND: When will you achieve this goal?

#4 A long-term goal for us as a couple is:

What will be the primary benefit of achieving this goal?

SPECIFIC: What exactly will you accomplish?

MEASURABLE: How will you and others know when you have reached your goal?

ATTAINABLE: Is attaining this goal realistic, and do you have the resources and ability to achieve the goal?

RELEVANT: Why is this goal important to you?

TIME-BOUND: When will you achieve this goal?

Share your four goals with your fiancé.

Discuss whether the short- and long-term goals for you as a couple need to involve the other person.

Be sure to encourage each other along the way. Ask how your fiancé best receives encouragement while pursuing goals.

Talk about the most helpful way to hold each other accountable with goals so they don't become points of tension in your relationship. Nagging and shame are never good routes to take when trying to motivate; encouragement is always the best route.

When we're together (or with our premarital counselor), be sure to talk about:

Date we discussed
this exercise:

EXERCISE THREE

Where I See Hope in Our Relationship

Hope is one of the most powerful forces in the world—and that is especially true in marriage. Hope can provide courage to make the right decisions, help you change your perspective, and give you strength to persevere through the difficult times all marriages experience.

In his book *The Hope Quotient*, Ray Johnston relays an insightful conversation with a very successful marriage counselor. The counselor's "secret" was helping couples experience hope. He said, "When couples get that 10 percent improvement, they get hope. *And when someone gets hope, anything is possible.*"[2]

When your marriage begins to drift off course and goes through a rough spot, you may feel like it's a crisis, but slight adjustments (10 percent) will help return your marriage to a place of health. Little changes can result in big hope that things will get better.

Where have you already experienced hope in your relationship?

Finish this sentence: I feel most hopeful about our relationship when …

When you experience difficulty and things feel like they're going sideways, what is the most productive way you can share those feelings with your fiancé, and, in the future, your spouse?

When we're together (or with our premarital counselor), be sure to talk about:

In marriage, you will have struggles, but possessing hope will give you the courage to keep moving ahead.

Edwin Louis Cole wrote, "You don't drown by falling in the water; you drown by staying there."[3]

Improving your situation or moving your life in a positive direction by just 10 percent can make all the difference.

Date we discussed this exercise:

CHAPTER THREE

IN-LAWS: YOU MARRY THE FAMILY

How deeply have you talked to each other about your soon-to-be extended family? Have you discussed how you will handle holidays? What are the unspoken traditions and expectations both families embrace during special occasions? How will you, as a couple, deal with crazy Uncle Phil? Every family has some weird cast members, and yours will too. You can't avoid family.

When you get married, you are morphing your relationship into a part of another family system that has its own established set of expectations, rules, opinions, and decisions—all of which have been around a lot longer than you and your fiancé have been together. This is one of the primary reasons in-law issues are a source of major conflict with couples.

Here is the reality you are facing with your in-laws: you can't ignore them or change them, so wisdom requires you to better understand them and your new role within the extended family.

Exercises

☐ **Your Family Map**

☐ **Holidays and Traditions**

☐ **Honest Conversations about Your In-Laws**

45

1

EXERCISE ONE

Your Family Map

Each person on this planet has a unique family genogram—a map of his or her family background, or what we refer to as a "life-script" in our *Getting Ready for Marriage* book.

When you marry, you will be writing a new script as a couple. To best understand where you want to go and who you want to be as a couple, you need to understand where you have been and how your family can and will influence your future.

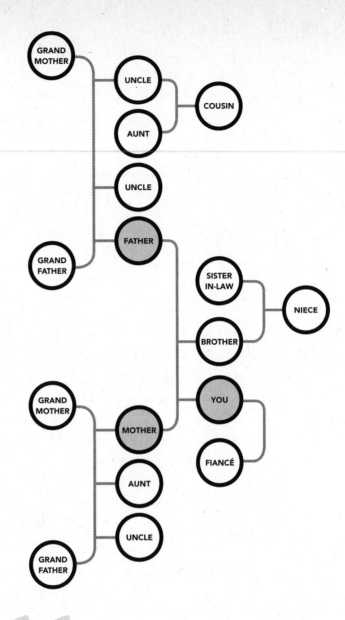

"A genogram (pronounced *jen-uh-gram*) is a picture of a family tree with detailed information about individuals. It contains more information than a traditional family tree so that the user can examine inherited patterns and psychological factors that impact relationships. Genograms allow counselors to quickly identify and understand various configurations in the person's family history that may influence them.

Look at the genogram to the left and then take time to draw your unique family map. Begin with your grandparents on both sides and work through your siblings. Include as much of the following information as you're able to find out:

- Name
- Dates of birth
- Marriages
- Divorces
- Noteworthy illnesses
- Deaths
- Alcoholism or drug use
- History of depression or mental illness
- Emotional problems
- Serious medical problems
- Conflict with the law
- Meaningful spiritual experiences
- Dominant tendencies (such as being overprotective, controlling, or expecting too much)

[handwritten notes: Mois mom, Todd grandma, ← dad, ← meis g-ma, Todd gpa, mei dad?, anxiety]

As you talk through the results from your family map, share what inspires you about your family history. Is there one person in particular whom you especially admire? Why?

What patterns or themes do you see?

What concerns you about your family?

How do you think your fiancé will respond to any family dysfunction or new family revelation you've uncovered?

When we're together (or with our premarital counselor), be sure to talk about:

"
We all have what is called a "family system," and that family system affects our values, beliefs, attitudes, priorities, and definitely our actions. To put it bluntly, your family has been the greatest contributing factor in why you are the way you are and who you are today.

What do you see as essential points of discussion for you and your fiancé after thinking more deeply about your family members and some of the patterns that emerged?

Date we discussed this exercise:

2

EXERCISE TWO

Holidays and Traditions

The phrase "You marry their family" is never truer than it is during holidays. Family members have patterns and traditions that hold special memories and feelings, making it difficult when someone makes a decision to disrupt what has been normal holiday procedure.

Change is inevitable, but misery is optional. We suggest you discuss family expectations early in your marriage. Clearly and carefully communicate with each other and your respective families about your plans for holidays. You probably won't please everyone, but you can work to make sure you're solidified in your actions as a newly married couple.

List each of your family's holidays and traditions (special birthdays, Christmas, Easter—basically, whatever holiday/tradition that has been meaningful to your family). As you consider your new marriage, take time to think through what your plans are going to be with these holiday celebrations and traditions. Are you going to preserve these actions and continue as normal? Or are you going to reject them? Start your own?

As you talk about these family traditions/expectations, realize that things will most likely change as you begin to form your own family values, experiences, and traditions. How are you going to communicate these changes to your family while trying to value and honor the meaning they have brought to your past? Don't forget to comment on what your family may view as an expectation and how you will handle those expectations as a newly married couple.

> " Once you establish new traditions and communicate them with love and respect, you'll most likely find that your families will accept the new reality with grace.

Holidays and Traditions

Currently, what is my family's expectation for my participation?

As of now, I think we will ...

Keep	X
Toss	_____
Adapt	_____
Undecided	_____

Christmas Eve: Attend church service, followed by Chinese dinner at home with friends and family where we each open one gift.

Comments/discussion:

"This is one of my favorite traditions. Be sure to talk to Cathy about how this will make her parents feel if we continue with this tradition and aren't with her parents on Christmas Eve. Or, do we invite them to join us?"

Holidays and Traditions

Currently, what is my family's expectation for my participation?

As of now, I think we will ...

Keep   _____

Toss   _____

Adapt   _____

Undecided   _____

Comments/discussion:

Holidays and Traditions

Currently, what is my family's expectation
for my participation?

As of now, I think we will ...

Keep   _____

Toss   _____

Adapt   _____

Undecided   _____

Comments/discussion:

Holidays and Traditions

Currently, what is my family's expectation for my participation?

As of now, I think we will ...

Keep   _____

Toss   _____

Adapt   _____

Undecided   _____

Comments/discussion:

Holidays and Traditions

Currently, what is my family's expectation for my participation?

As of now, I think we will ...

Keep   _____

Toss   _____

Adapt   _____

Undecided   _____

When we're together (or with our premarital counselor), be sure to talk about:

Comments/discussion:

Date we discussed this exercise:

EXERCISE THREE

Honest Conversations about Your In-Laws

You may be marrying the child of Mr. and Mrs. Wonderful, or you may be marrying the child of Cruella De Vil and Freddy Krueger. Either way, your in-laws will have an impact on your marriage. The following questions are intended to guide you through honest and helpful conversations—not accusatory statements. Be gentle and kind, but also be honest as you think through your answers.

Evaluate How Your Parents Will Be as In-Laws

What special concerns do you have about your parents as in-laws?

How involved do you want your parents to be in your life after marriage? Do you see any ways this may be difficult for your spouse?

How difficult will it be for you to "leave and cleave" with your fiancé? What might make this transition easier?

Maybe your family is seriously broken. One of the common reasons couples seek counseling is to learn how to respond to deep problems within their family systems.

Evaluate Your Fiancé's Family

Fill in the blanks:

I am most looking forward to _____
in regard to your family.

I am most concerned about _____
in regard to your family.

My expectations about your parents' involvement in our lives are:

When we're together (or with our premarital counselor), be sure to talk about:

General In-Law Questions

How often will you see your in-laws?

How will you deal with an in-law who expresses financial or physical need?

Date we discussed this exercise:

" Couples encounter trouble when they don't talk about issues or develop boundaries together. If you are dealing with a troubled family member who seems to be getting in the way of your marriage, reach out to a mentor or counselor for support to ensure that, at all costs, you keep your marriage healthy.

" If you need help developing healthy boundaries with troubled family members, do whatever it takes to safeguard your marriage.

CHAPTER FOUR

COMMUNICATION: THE FASTEST ROUTE TO CONNECTION

Strong communication is the foundation of a stable marriage and the key that unlocks the door to a healthy, happy, and secure relationship. A marriage that has healthy communication requires hard work and the development of skills that are practiced and evaluated regularly. The exercises in this chapter are meant to enhance your communication with each other and bring insight to other topics that will strengthen your relationship.

> **Marriage research reveals that 86 percent of all marriages that derail place "poor communication" as the primary reason. In a recent poll, almost all who rate their communication as "excellent" are happily married. The poll concluded: "In an era of increasingly fragile marriages, a couple's ability to communicate is the single most important contributor to a stable and satisfying marriage."[1]**

Exercises

- ☐ Your Personality Inventory
- ☐ Replenishing Your Relationship with A.W.E.
- ☐ Blocks to Healthy Communication

EXERCISE ONE

Your Personality Inventory

This is a very simple exercise designed to produce thoughtful conversation. Don't overthink it! Circle the number that most closely identifies you and your fiancé with one of the headings. Go with your gut—the quicker you choose a number and circle it, the more accurate it will probably be.

> **Many aspects of your relationship may feel easy and natural during the pre-engagement and engagement season. But fast-forward six months to a year after the wedding and that is when cracks in the communication armor may appear.**

Answer each question about yourself first (circle the number on the "Me" line).

Immediately repeat the exercise and answer where you perceive your fiancé to be (circle the number on the "Fiancé" line).

Note: There are no right or wrong answers. This exercise is intended to help you talk about how you perceive yourself, how you perceive your fiancé, and how those perceptions are similar or different.

Have fun! Again, don't overthink it. Just go.

Extrovert/Outgoing								Introvert/Reserved	
Me: 1	2	3	4	5	6	7	8	9	10
Fiancé: 1	2	3	4	5	6	7	8	9	10

Neat								Messy	
Me: 1	2	3	4	5	6	7	8	9	10
Fiancé: 1	2	3	4	5	6	7	8	9	10

Spiritual								Not Spiritual	
Me: 1	2	3	4	5	6	7	8	9	10
Fiancé: 1	2	3	4	5	6	7	8	9	10

Passive								Aggressive	
Me: 1	2	3	4	5	6	7	8	9	10
Fiancé: 1	2	3	4	5	6	7	8	9	10

Spender		Saver
Me: 1 2 3 4 5 6 7 8 9 10		
Fiancé: 1 2 3 4 5 6 7 8 9 10		

Deep		Not So Deep
Me: 1 2 3 4 5 6 7 8 9 10		
Fiancé: 1 2 3 4 5 6 7 8 9 10		

Calm/Easygoing		Anxious/High-Strung
Me: 1 2 3 4 5 6 7 8 9 10		
Fiancé: 1 2 3 4 5 6 7 8 9 10		

Risk Taker		Cautious
Me: 1 2 3 4 5 6 7 8 9 10		
Fiancé: 1 2 3 4 5 6 7 8 9 10		

Talker		Listener
Me: 1 2 3 4 5 6 7 8 9 10		
Fiancé: 1 2 3 4 5 6 7 8 9 10		

Perfectionist		Nonperfectionist
Me: 1 2 3 4 5 6 7 8 9 10		
Fiancé: 1 2 3 4 5 6 7 8 9 10		

Makes Logical Decisions		Makes Emotional Decisions
Me: 1 2 3 4 5 6 7 8 9 10		
Fiancé: 1 2 3 4 5 6 7 8 9 10		

Realist		Idealist
Me: 1 2 3 4 5 6 7 8 9 10		
Fiancé: 1 2 3 4 5 6 7 8 9 10		

Leader		Follower
Me: 1 2 3 4 5 6 7 8 9 10		
Fiancé: 1 2 3 4 5 6 7 8 9 10		

Homebody		Adventurer
Me: 1 2 3 4 5 6 7 8 9 10		
Fiancé: 1 2 3 4 5 6 7 8 9 10		

Planned		Spontaneous
Me: 1 2 3 4 5 6 7 8 9 10		
Fiancé: 1 2 3 4 5 6 7 8 9 10		

Circle the top three from the list that make you think, *Hmmm, I wonder how that will play out long-term in our marriage?*

Why do these concern you?

**What specific questions do you want to ask your fiancé
when you get together to discuss this?**

When you're together with time to discuss:

Compare your answers.

Understand that these ratings are not meant to describe the truth or reality, but are meant only to reveal perceptions. Perception is not necessarily the truth, but it can still be valid. Be sure to discuss the answers where you see yourself significantly different from how your fiancé sees you.

Note the places where you disagree with your fiancé's self-assessment. As you move forward in discussion, please commit to being gentle and kind. Talking about how you view each other differently can be a potentially hurtful and difficult conversation. But it's important that you learn to explain to each other why you perceive him or her the way you do.

What did you learn about your fiancé from this exercise?

How will you feel if your fiancé never changes in one of the areas where your perceptions are different?

Based on this conversation, is there anything you need to begin working on in yourself? If so, what is it?

When we're together (or with our premarital counselor), be sure to talk about:

Date we discussed this exercise:

EXERCISE TWO

Replenishing Your Relationship with A.W.E.

One of the most effective ways to communicate with your spouse is by setting an atmosphere of A.W.E. in your home. A.W.E. stands for *Affection, Warmth,* and *Encouragement.* Daily doses of genuine A.W.E. guarantee better communication. When you learn to deposit these positive actions into your marriage on a regular basis, you'll find that the emotional withdrawals that accompany conflict and tension won't feel as harsh.

AFFECTION refers to the basic human need to love and be loved. Affection is not only about romance, but it also includes nonsexual touch, such as hugs, holding hands, sitting close on the couch, cuddling, and brushing a hand across his or her back when you walk by. Affection is a nonverbal form of communication and one of the most powerful demonstrators of love.

WARMTH is about setting a warm tone in the home. When communication is welcoming, warm, and cheerful, the relationship can thrive. When communication is negative, critical, and full of complaints, the relationship can turn cold. You won't be able to avoid conflict in your marriage, but a commitment to warmth will make arguments easier to deal with.

> **As newlyweds, you'll need to figure out what it takes to create a warm atmosphere in your home. Couples who make their home a sanctuary are more successful in communication.**

ENCOURAGEMENT builds your fiancé up and helps maintain a sense of emotional security. A steady diet of kind, encouraging, and empowering words can create a strong sense of confidence within your fiancé.

> **You will have a healthy marriage when you learn to use your words to engage in intimate conversations, share feelings, express needs, inform your spouse, and bring delight.**

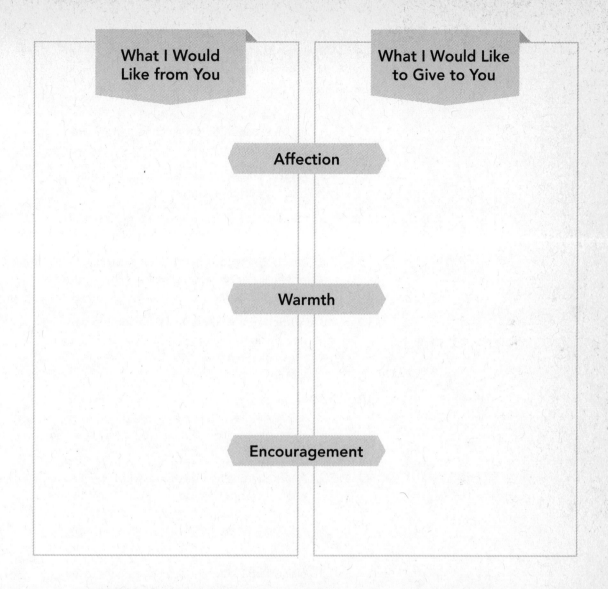

What I Would Like from You	What I Would Like to Give to You
Affection	
Warmth	
Encouragement	

When we're together (or with our premarital counselor), be sure to talk about:

Date we discussed this exercise:

EXERCISE THREE

Blocks to Healthy Communication

Everyone has the capacity to block healthy and productive communication. Oftentimes you may not even know you're blocking communication because you've learned habits and patterns that feel so natural to you.

Take time to look through this list of some of the most common blocks to communication and see which ones apply to you and your fiancé. When you are able to identify your common way of blocking communication, you will be more effective in communication.

Which of these most clearly describes your tendency to impact good communication? Mark the ones that most apply to you and your fiancé.

Communication Blocks

You   Fiancé

○ ○ **Hungry:** Hungry people tend to be grumpier. Getting some food may change how you communicate.

○ ○ **Angry:** Shared or repressed anger shuts down healthy communication.

○ ○ **Lonely:** Loneliness tends to trigger self-pity and can alter effective communication.

○ ○ **Tired:** When you are tired, exhausted, or physically depleted, defense mechanisms go up and the ability to think rationally goes down.

○ ○ **Addictions:** Addicts typically don't experience healthy intimacy or communication because they value relationships and communication less than their addiction.

○ ○ **Technology:** Computers, phones, texting, social media, and constant attention to them can become a distraction and a way to avoid healthy communication.

○ ○ **Avoidance:** When a couple avoids dealing with conflict through communication, it results in stockpiling hurt. When you hold on to hurt, it releases bitterness and resentment into the relationship.

○ ○ **Negativity:** Nagging and negativity cause the recipient to withdraw and be passive in communication.

○ ○ **Mind Reading:** Hinting and hoping your fiancé knows what you're thinking is a poor form of communication.

○ ○ **Attacking:** Blaming, shaming, yelling, and bringing up the past are all destructive forms of communication that simply don't work.

○ ○ **Superiority:** Arrogance and a superior attitude and tone are not only self-centered, but they can also quickly shut down communication.

What other blocks have you observed in couples or experienced in your past that aren't mentioned? Share your findings with each other.

Discuss your strategy for how you will approach conflict in the future based on what you've learned.

" As you pause to think about your communication patterns, you must also pay special attention to the fact that it's not just about the words you use; it's also about the tone that projects your words. Sarcasm, shaming, pessimism, negativity, whining, and insincerity are just as much about tone as words.

When we're together (or with our premarital counselor), be sure to talk about:

How will you approach a conflict that you both know is happening but neither is talking about?

What will happen when you hurt your fiancé but you are unaware of the pain and damage you caused?

How will you approach your fiancé when you've been hurt but he or she doesn't seem to care in the way you want?

Date we discussed this exercise:

" Most engaged couples don't often think about being lonely because there is so much happening with wedding plans. Actually, wedding busyness can mask loneliness.

CHAPTER FIVE

CONFLICT: THE RULES OF ENGAGEMENT

All couples will experience conflict. (If you don't, there are probably issues you are simply avoiding.)

While you can't escape conflict in marriage, you can learn to manage it so it doesn't cause damage. Good conflict-management skills begin *before* you get married. If your relationship is filled with constant conflict now and it's not dealt with in a healthy manner, you could be in trouble before you even say "I do."

Conflict can become an ingredient in the development of deeper intimacy. Again, the important issue is not *if* you have conflict but *how* you deal with your conflict *when* it arrives.

> **Conflict is inevitable! It's not unusual for couples to enter into marriage believing the lie that conflict shouldn't exist in a healthy marriage. Don't believe it! When two individuals join their lives together, they are bound to bump into issues and rub each other the wrong way at times.**

Exercises

- ☐ The Conflict Dance
- ☐ The Power of an Apology
- ☐ Conflict Triggers

EXERCISE ONE

The Conflict Dance

The two diagrams shown in this exercise are from our book *Getting Ready for Marriage*. At a quick glance you'll notice that both the Negative and Positive Conflict Dances begin with a specific tension. What makes them different is the direction the conflict takes. These two distinct paths will lead your conflict toward different outcomes—one of resolution or one of additional tension.

" Problems, disagreements, and tension are inevitable—but misery is optional.

Name at least one conflict you've experienced when you took the "Negative" route and one conflict when you took the "Positive" route. Then, looking at the diagrams, write how you handled them and how you could have been more effective.

The goal for this exercise isn't for you to relive the tension; it's designed to help you reflect on and evaluate the steps you took.

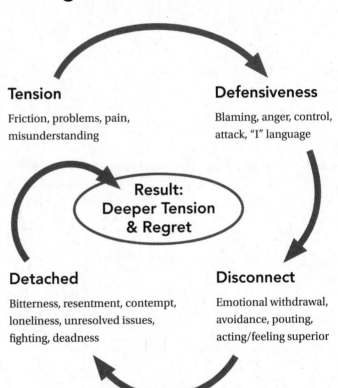

Negative Conflict Dance

Tension
Friction, problems, pain, misunderstanding

Defensiveness
Blaming, anger, control, attack, "I" language

Result: Deeper Tension & Regret

Detached
Bitterness, resentment, contempt, loneliness, unresolved issues, fighting, deadness

Disconnect
Emotional withdrawal, avoidance, pouting, acting/feeling superior

" If your primary intent is to defend yourself and win, you won't get to resolution as a couple. If your intent during conflict is to grow and learn, you must drop your defenses and pride, and make your issue the target.

Negative Conflict Dance

Name your conflict:

_____

Using the illustration to the left as a model, describe your feelings at each stage.

TENSION: What triggered the conflict? How did you feel at this point? What resulting actions did you take? What could you have done differently or better?

DEFENSIVENESS: What did your defensiveness look like? How did you feel at this point in the conflict? What resulting actions did you take? What could you have done differently or better?

DISCONNECT: When you disconnected, what form did it take? How did you feel at this point in the conflict? What resulting actions did you take? What could you have done differently or better?

DETACHED: What did your detachment look like? How did you feel at this point in the conflict? What resulting actions did you take? What could you have done differently or better?

RESULT: Deeper Tension and Regret. How did this tension finally get resolved? What did you learn about yourself and your fiancé based on the actions you took?

> Happily married couples don't necessarily have fewer problems; they simply have learned how to share their feelings and opinions during a disagreement and still make their spouse feel loved and valued.

Positive Conflict Dance

"We"
Assumes responsibility and works together to resolve the issue

Tension
Friction, problem, pain, misunderstanding

Result: Authentic Oneness & Feeling Loved

Connected
Resolution without win/lose, sense of well-being (i.e., "**all** is okay!"), new learnings about each other, peace

Positive Conflict Dance

Name your conflict:

_____

Using the illustration to the left as a model, describe your feelings at each stage.

TENSION: What triggered the conflict? How did you feel at this point? What resulting actions did you take? Is there anything you could have done better at this point?

"WE": How did you turn the tension into an opportunity to work together to solve the issue? Is there anything you could have done better at this point?

CONNECTED: How did this bring you closer together? Is there anything you could have done better at this point?

RESULT: Authentic Oneness and Feeling Loved.
At the conclusion of this conflict, how was your intimacy
for each other enhanced?

> How you deal with conflict
> will be a huge factor in
> determining the health and
> vitality of your marriage.

We suggest you not only talk about this as a couple, but you also share this exercise with whoever is
doing your premarital counseling.

When we're together (or with our premarital counselor), be sure to talk about:

Date we discussed
this exercise:

EXERCISE TWO

The Power of an Apology

It is so much easier to deal with conflict when you offer a sincere, heartfelt apology. We have found that the three types of apologies we present are not only powerful but also offer a breakthrough toward deeper intimacy in marriage.

> **It's helpful to your future to learn that every conflict doesn't need a winner or a loser.**

REGRET: Offering regret and remorse for causing hurt.

"I spoke in anger and not only did I not mean the hurtful things I said, but I am deeply sorry for saying them. Please forgive me."

RESPONSIBILITY: Taking full responsibility for an action, word, or tone.

"I blew it. I tried to make my issue about you. It wasn't. I caused you pain, and I am deeply sorry for offending you. Please forgive me."

REMEDY: While you can't always undo the past, you can often repair the wrong.

"I was wrong. I can see how I hurt you. I need to make it right and will do so by_____. Please forgive me."

When sincere apologies become part of your relationship, you will experience much-needed healing and reconciliation. So much pain can be avoided if one of you admits your pride, embraces humility, and offers an apology.

Using the three types of apologies as a model, write your fiancé three short apology notes. If you can't think of a current issue requiring an apology, go ahead and bring up a past issue that has been resolved so that you can practice. This is an important exercise because the process of articulating an apology serves as a significant action in overcoming conflict.

> **Don't start with the other person. Start by looking in the mirror and reflecting deeply on where the anger originated.**

REGRET:

RESPONSIBILITY:

REMEDY:

Share your apology examples with your fiancé.

How did you feel listening to your fiancé share his or her apology?

Why do you think this will be easy or difficult for you in your relationship?

" **Be liberal with your apologies, and you will be able to love more deeply. Conflict will be much easier: there is almost nothing as powerful as a sincere apology.**

Take some time to talk about how important apologizing will be moving forward.

When we're together (or with our premarital counselor), be sure to talk about:

Date we discussed this exercise:

EXERCISE THREE

3

Conflict Triggers

To create a healthy relationship, it's important to recognize your conflict triggers. To the right is a partial list of possible areas and reasons for conflict. Rank the top-five potential triggers that are most likely to appear in your relationship. Place a "1" by the most obvious, and then work your way down to number "5."

> **Some conflict will appear in your marriage because of your deepening intimacy. You will begin to think about how much more is at stake with your relationship.**

Conflict Triggers

_____ Children (how many and when?)

_____ Money

_____ In-laws

_____ Jealousy

_____ Addictions

_____ Raising children

_____ Spiritual life

_____ Politics

_____ Opposite-sex relationships

_____ Job

_____ Hobbies

_____ Sex

_____ Chores around the house

_____ Tardiness

_____ Television, phone, computer, or other technology

_____ Driving

_____ Bad habits and annoying behaviors

_____ Sports

_____ Shopping

_____ Friends

_____ Wedding planning

_____ Career

> **There is compelling evidence that phones, computers, and tinkering on social media can not only trigger conflict but also become a block to good communication.**

_____ Time spent together

_____ Holidays

_____ Communication patterns

_____ Entertainment

_____ Cooking

_____ Pets

_____ Honeymoon

_____ Cleanliness

_____ Use of time

_____ Anger

_____ Passive-aggressive behavior

_____ Other _____

_____ Other _____

_____ Other _____

_____ Other _____

Begin your discussion by saying, "While I'd like to hope this won't be an issue, I can see _____ becoming a point of tension in our relationship because _____."

When you hear your fiancé share what his or her top triggers are and why, how does it make you feel? Are there any surprises?

Discuss how you plan to defuse and resolve these situations when they arise.

End your time together by renewing your commitment to not ignore your tension and to be open about your feelings while resolving conflicts.

When we're together (or with our premarital counselor), be sure to talk about:

Date we discussed this exercise:

CHAPTER SIX

FINANCES: THE BEST THINGS IN LIFE ARE NOT THINGS

No doubt about it, finances, debt, and spending habits can invite tension into a marriage. Whether you are rich or poor, managing money and living within your means is one of the most important factors in determining the success of your marriage.

Many couples begin their marriage before planning how they will handle finances, which can lead to poor decisions. But couples who learn to develop a workable plan, live by a budget, deal with debt, delay gratification, and set themselves up to give and save will enjoy a healthier marriage.

The big question is: Will you choose spending and debt, or delayed gratification and a responsible budget? If you haven't already discussed this, you need to give this question serious consideration and then plot your steps to ensure long-term success.

Exercises

☐ **Your Budget**

☐ **Creating a Debt-Reduction Plan**

☐ **The Big Ten: Just Say Yes!**

1

EXERCISE ONE

Your Budget

One of the key elements of a financially healthy marriage is a simple concept: spend less money than you make. Of course, it's easier said than done.

In order to do so consistently, you'll need to create a realistic budget and then learn to live by that budget.

A healthy first step toward budgeting as a couple is to spend time updating your personal budget. Do so in pencil first, or if you budget on your computer, create a new version that you don't mind making more changes to, so that when you meet together, you can combine your numbers for a more accurate combined budget.

To the right is a budget template we've created to help you make your first budget as a couple. Work through this during your time together, remembering that it doesn't have to be perfect on the first try. The important thing is that you communicate clearly about your expectations and desires, and come to an agreement before you decide on any particular number. For a downloadable version of this budget worksheet, go to www.gettingreadyformarriage.com/worksheets.

> **You won't know if you are succeeding financially if you don't create a measurable budget to keep you accountable. While it may seem like a budget is reducing your freedom, it's actually freeing to know what you can afford.**

Monthly Budget Worksheet

Income:

Wages (combined)	$	
Extra income	$	
Total monthly income	$	
Total annual income	$	

Expenses:

Home

Mortgage or rent	$	
Homeowners or renters insurance	$	
Property taxes	$	
Home repairs and maintenance	$	
Dues or assoc. fees	$	
Home improvement	$	
Misc.	$	

Utilities

Telephone	$	
Natural gas or oil	$	
Water and sewer	$	
Trash collection	$	
Electric	$	
Internet/cable	$	
Netflix or other subscriptions	$	

Food

Groceries $ ☐

Eating out, snacks, coffee $ ☐

Auto

Auto payments (combined) $ ☐

Auto insurance (combined) $ ☐

Gas/oil $ ☐

Auto repairs/maintenance $ ☐

Other transportation (tolls/taxis/bus/subway) $ ☐

License and registration $ ☐

Other $ ☐

Entertainment

Vacations $ ☐

Movies $ ☐

Hobbies $ ☐

Sporting events $ ☐

Theater $ ☐

Concerts $ ☐

CDs/DVDs/downloads $ ☐

Apps $ ☐

Investments

Savings $ ☐

401(k) $ ☐

Stocks/bonds/mutual funds/college fund $ ☐

Giving/Donations

Tithe $ [____]

Charities $ [____]

Clothing (combined) $ [____]

Pets

Food and grooming $ [____]

Vet $ [____]

Grooming

Hair/makeup $ [____]

Toiletries $ [____]

Manicures/pedicures $ [____]

Debt

Credit cards $ [____]

Student loans $ [____]

Debt reduction $ [____]

Other debt $ [____]

Family Obligations

Day care/babysitting $ [____]

Child support/alimony $ [____]

Health and Medical

Insurance $ _____

Unreimbursed medical insurance $ _____

Counseling $ _____

Medication $ _____

Dentist $ _____

Fitness $ _____

Other _____ $ _____

Gifts

Christmas $ _____

Birthdays $ _____

Anniversaries $ _____

Other _____ $ _____

Other

Dry cleaning/laundry $ _____

Computer expenses $ _____

Subscriptions and dues $ _____

Total Annual Income: _____

Total Annual Expenses: _____

After working through the details of budgeting, what were your major observations and questions?

What are the primary financial issues that need to be addressed immediately? Write them down with completion dates.

What financial concerns do you have for your future?

> **The question for you to consider essentially boils down to what kind of pain you would rather experience with your finances: Do you want to experience the pain of discipline or the pain of regret?**

What is your plan to make sure both of you are involved in financial decisions? If you don't have a plan, be sure to make one. (Read chapter 6 of our book *Getting Ready for Marriage* for more specifics.)

When we're together (or with our premarital counselor), be sure to talk about:

We strongly suggest that you meet with someone who has more wisdom and experience with finances to have them review your budget. Who might that person be? When will you contact that person?

" Making a commitment to live within your budget is the best form of accountability to help you reach your financial goals. Don't get married without making a commitment to create a budget and stick to it.

Date we discussed this exercise:

② EXERCISE TWO

Creating a Debt-Reduction Plan

If you are not carrying any debt, then you get a free pass on this exercise. Congratulations! Very few couples enter into marriage without some form of debt. Developing and following a debt-reduction plan is one of the very best actions you can do to move toward financial freedom in your marriage. The time to create a debt plan is before you get married.

> " It's quite simple: happy couples tend to deal with their finances well, and unhappy couples tend not to handle their finances well.

Four Steps to Creating Your Personal Debt-Reduction Plan

1. Make a budget and commit to it. Make sure you have already created a budget that includes a specific amount toward paying off your debt as quickly as possible. (If not, be sure to complete exercise 1 in this chapter.)

☐ Yes! We have a workable budget and we are willing to do whatever it takes to follow our budget. (Put a check in the box if this applies to you.)

> " The pain of financial discipline might mean you will need to make some difficult sacrifices and choose not to live at a level you can't afford.

2. List all your debt. Here are two options to consider when creating your list: (1) start from highest amount owed down to the least. Or (2) list debt by highest interest rate. There's no one right way to do this; simply choose which of these two options is most clear to you. Be sure to list all debt—no matter how small.

List Debt (step 2)	Monthly Payment (step 3—see below)

We like the clarity and simplicity of Dave Ramsey's *"Seven Baby Steps"*[1] to debt reduction.

STEP ONE: Put away $1,000 in an emergency fund

STEP TWO: Pay off all debt

STEP THREE: Secure three to six months of your budget in savings

STEP FOUR: Invest 15 percent of household income into Roth IRAs and pretax retirement

STEP FIVE: Pursue college funding for your children

STEP SIX: Pay off your home early

STEP SEVEN: Build wealth and give

3. Create a clear plan of debt reduction. Know how much you will pay off every month and stick to the plan. Next to your specific debt (above), come up with a reasonable amount that you can pay every month to reduce your debt. It would be wise to begin working on your debt reduction now … yes, before you get married.

If you need ideas on how to reduce cost with some simple thoughts, see page 132 in the book *Getting Ready for Marriage.*

4. Pay your bills. A common mistake many newlyweds make is to create a debt-reduction plan and then not follow through by making consistent, monthly payments. By doing this, they simply create more debt.

Monthly Financial Accountability Questions

Are we following our budget and debt-reduction plan?

Was there any bill that we were unable to pay this month?

Do we have any concerns about next month's budget? If so, what change do we need to make to our budget/spending in order to stick to our plan?

When your debt plan has worked and you are living debt-free, take time to celebrate and do something fun. Be sure you don't go into more debt to finance your celebration!

List some ideas for how we might celebrate when we are debt-free:

> "You can create strong security by choosing not to live on the edge of financial disaster. The pain of disciplined spending and saving is definitely the way to begin your marriage.

When we're together (or with our premarital counselor), be sure to talk about:

Date we discussed this exercise:

3

EXERCISE THREE

The Big Ten: Just Say Yes!

This is a simple exercise. The goal is to be able to say yes to each of the following statements. When you can honestly answer in the affirmative, move on to the next statement. If your answer is anything other than yes, discuss what needs to happen in order to get to that answer.

"Fact: financial issues are one of the most common sources of stress for couples.

1. We have taken time to create a realistic budget.

   O yes   O no   O need more discussion

2. We have decided on a percentage of our income that we will put aside for retirement.

   O yes   O no   O need more discussion

3. We have decided on a percentage of our income that we will put aside for savings.

   O yes   O no   O need more discussion

4. We have decided on a percentage of our income that we will put aside for charitable giving.

   O yes   O no   O need more discussion

5. We have disclosed to each other every debt and asset we have.

   O yes   O no   O need more discussion

6. We will have differences in how we spend money, but we have discussed how we will work them out.

   O yes   O no   O need more discussion

7. We have decided on purchases we are willing to go into debt for, such as a home, car, school tuition, vacation, or new computer.

   ○ yes   ○ no   ○ need more discussion

8. We know who will track and reconcile our monthly finances.

   ○ yes   ○ no   ○ need more discussion

9. We have decided the amount we can spend on our own without having to ask the other person for permission.

   ○ yes   ○ no   ○ need more discussion

10. We completely trust each other to make wise financial decisions.

    ○ yes   ○ no   ○ need more discussion

Make sure you take time to discuss any issue that doesn't receive a "yes."

Financial stressors impact couples regardless of their income level. You may be wealthy, but you can still become *relationally* poor in your marriage if you don't handle your finances well.

Date we discussed this exercise:

CHAPTER SEVEN

SEXUALITY: THE NAKED TRUTH

Sex is sacred. Sex is important. Sex is fun. Sex is God's design for incredible physical intimacy. But sex can also be confusing, divisive, and can trigger painful memories from the past. Bottom line: sex brings with it all kinds of emotions.

Regardless of your experience or lack of experience, dealing with your sexuality is an important ingredient in a successful marriage. Sex holds the potential for great joy as well as great harm. Statistics revealing the top reasons for divorce put sex-related issues near the top of the list.[1] How can this be? It seems like such an easy and pleasurable act, so what makes it so difficult?

Many factors can impact whether sex brings you closer together or divides you as a married couple; therefore, it's important for you to openly talk about your fears, your past, your expectations, and your needs. Those discussions should continue long past your completion of this workbook, but these exercises will help you get started.

Exercises

☐ The Sex Questionnaire

☐ The Purity Code Challenge

☐ The Five Sex Needs of Men and Women

> **God intended sex to be beautiful, pleasurable, and to create oneness within marriage. Sex wasn't *accidentally* discovered by a caveman and cavewoman who were out wrestling.**

EXERCISE ONE

The Sex Questionnaire

Answer the questions, and then openly discuss your answers during your time together. Although talking about sexuality can be awkward, we believe it is critical to your future and to fulfillment within your marriage. We strongly encourage you to seek wisdom from a trusted premarital counselor as you have these discussions.

How did you first hear about sex? From parents or a friend? At school or online?

How old were you when you first understood the basics of sexual relations?

As you were growing up, did you have a positive or negative opinion of sex and your sexuality? Why?

Do you believe you are carrying any sexual baggage into this relationship? If so, how do you think that baggage could impact your marriage?

Have you ever been sexually abused? If so, have you spent significant time with a counselor dealing with that issue? (If not, we urge you to seek counseling *before* you marry.)

Are there any physical relationship experiences from your past you haven't dealt with yet in your current relationship that could trigger shame in the future?

What has been your experience with pornography?

How would you feel if you found out your fiancé is currently engaged in pornography?

If you or your fiancé is involved in pornography, how will you provide grace and accountability moving forward?

"One of the major issues we're discovering in premarital and marital counseling is pornography—from minor dabbling to full-on addiction. What was once viewed as a sexual experience that "wasn't hurting anyone" has now morphed into a harmful sexual problem that's ruining marriages. DON'T HIDE THIS ISSUE IF YOU ARE STRUGGLING WITH IT.

Would you be willing to abstain from sexual intercourse until the day of your wedding? If not, why? For more information on sex before marriage, see pages 149–152 in our book *Getting Ready for Marriage*.

When we're together (or with our premarital counselor), be sure to talk about:

Are you aware that the word *gospel* means "good news," and the good news about God is that there is forgiveness from your past because of Jesus Christ? How might forgiveness need to play a part in your current relationship?

Some individuals bring sexual issues into marriage because they haven't been given healthy sex education. They've heard that sex is "dirty, rotten, and awful … so save it till marriage for the one you love." Really? What kind of message is that?

God isn't antisex. Nothing could be further from the truth. Although our culture has tried to redefine the purpose of sex, God's intention is and always has been for a husband and wife to enjoy great intimacy and beauty in the expression of their sexuality.

If you have not read chapter 7 in our book *Getting Ready for Marriage*, we urge you to read it and discover the science behind and hidden consequences of cohabitation. It will also help you gain a healthy perspective of your sexuality as well as discover the beauty of God's plan for sex.

Date we discussed this exercise:

EXERCISE TWO

> **The safest road to emotional, physical, and even spiritual intimacy is purity and fidelity.**

The Purity Code Challenge

The odds for a successful marriage move from *mediocre* to *almost impossible* if you don't both commit to live with sexual integrity. This is an intentional commitment to be sexually faithful to your spouse *without compromise.*

A commitment to purity is broader than just being physically faithful to your fiancé or spouse. It includes your heart, mind, and even your eyes. Issues connected to emotional affairs (your heart), pornography (your mind), and allowing your gaze to linger on someone of the opposite sex (your eyes) are highly damaging to a marriage.

To help couples with this commitment, we have developed the Purity Code Challenge. It's a simple, biblical commitment to each other to help you live with sexual integrity and maintain a strong marital bond. Are you willing to commit your life and your relationship to the Purity Code?

Do you not know that your bodies are temples of the Holy Spirit, who is in you, whom you have received from God? You are not your own; you were bought at a price. Therefore honor God with your bodies. (1 Corinthians 6:19–20)

The Purity Code Pledge

In honor of God, my family, and my future spouse, I commit my life to sexual purity.

This involves:

Honoring God with my body.
Renewing my mind for the good.
Turning my eyes from worthless things.
Guarding my heart above all else.

Signature _____ Date _____

Signature _____ Date _____

If you are courageous enough to commit to the Purity Code Challenge, sign and date it. If your fiancé is willing to do the same, have him or her sign it in your workbook. (If your fiancé is not willing to commit to this challenge, that should be seen as a red flag, which will require additional conversation and counseling.)

Finish the following sentence during conversation with your fiancé: "Because of your pledge to purity in our relationship, it makes me feel _____."

The more specific you are when you answer, the better.

Take time to identify what it means to you to:

Honor God with your body:

Renew your mind:

Turn your eyes from worthless things:

Guard your heart:

When we're together (or with our premarital counselor), be sure to talk about:

Date we discussed this exercise:

3
EXERCISE THREE

The Five Sex Needs of Men and Women

Marriage experts Gary and Barb Rosberg wrote a book called *The 5 Sex Needs of Men and Women*.[2] In it, they provide helpful and surprising thoughts about how men and women have different sexual needs. Review these needs, reflect on them by answering the provided questions, and then discuss your answers with your fiancé.

Men Need	Women Need
1. Mutual satisfaction	1. Affirmation
2. Connection	
3. Responsiveness of wife	3. Nonsexual touch
4. Initiation of wife	4. Spiritual intimacy
5. Affirmation	5. Romance

MUTUAL SATISFACTION: Desire that they both experience enjoyment and satisfaction through sex.

AFFIRMATION: Building up her self-esteem. Kind words. Pointing out what she does right. Appreciating her.

CONNECTION: Emotional closeness. Understanding. Security in their commitment to each other. Most women want to feel the connection before sex, while most men feel it afterward.

RESPONSIVENESS: Wants his wife to respond sexually; to want him. It builds his confidence.

NONSEXUAL TOUCH: Physical touch that isn't connected to sex. Holding hands. Snuggling. Any physical sign that communicates she is special.

INITIATION: Shows that she cares about their sex life, his needs, and what's very important to him.

SPIRITUAL INTIMACY: A mutual desire to be close to God and seek God's direction for the marriage. Connecting to the deepest parts of who she is—the spiritual part.

AFFIRMATION: Using words that build him up—especially in regard to his sexuality. Encourage and appreciate him.

ROMANCE: Not equated with sex. For women, romance is something you do to express the love you feel.

As you can tell from the needs list, a husband's and wife's intimacy needs are not all physical—emotional and spiritual needs are vital too.

Did any of these sex needs surprise you? Which ones? Why?

Many couples have trouble talking about physical intimacy. On a scale from 1 to 5 (1 being poor and 5 being great), how would you rate your ability to talk about sexual intimacy with your fiancé?

There are exceptions to this, but most women feel emotional connection *before* sex, and most men feel an intense emotional connection *after* sex. How could this create tension in your relationship?

What type of emotional connection do you want from your fiancé that may enhance your physical intimacy in marriage?

> If you are too busy to emotionally connect with each other or have any meaningful nonsexual interaction, then you'll probably be too busy to have a good sexual relationship. Good sex begins before you ever get to the bedroom.

My greatest anticipation for our sexual relationship is:

My greatest fear about our sexual relationship is:

My biggest questions about our sexual relationship are:

The wonderful mystery surrounding sex is that you won't become an expert overnight. Figuring out how to please each other sexually throughout marriage is a beautiful gift that God gives you. Even if you have fears and questions, you'll be okay; you have years to learn.

When we're together (or with our premarital counselor), be sure to talk about:

Date we discussed this exercise:

CHAPTER EIGHT

SPIRITUAL INTIMACY: THE POWER OF COMPATIBILITY

When a husband and wife are on the same page spiritually, they have a greater chance of creating a successful marriage. A high level of spiritual agreement equals a greater level of marital satisfaction. We suggest that if you are not compatible in your spiritual beliefs and practices, take time *before* marriage to talk things over with your premarital counselor.

Too many couples put off important conversations about faith and end up with deep sadness later in their marriage as a result. This is too important of an issue to hope that it will change once you're married. Strong marriages aren't built on hope.

> "Spiritual intimacy is often one of the least-developed areas of a relationship for couples, and yet it's one of the most important issues in determining your marital happiness.

Exercises

- ☐ Your Spiritual Journey
- ☐ Committing to the "Closer Challenge"
- ☐ Finding a Marriage Mentor Couple

EXERCISE ONE

Your Spiritual Journey

Spiritual compatibility is much more important than many couples imagine. When couples don't align with similar faith values or share expressions of faith, it adds tension to the marriage. It can also create an uncomfortable environment for children who grow up watching their parents divided on faith issues.

Reflect on your own spiritual journey, and then discuss your expectations and the importance of spiritual issues in your future marriage.

How would you describe your spiritual upbringing?

Who is your most important spiritual role model?

How would you describe your current relationship with God?

"In addition to growing spiritually as a couple, you need to be focused on growing as individuals. You shouldn't demand that your spouse fulfill needs that really should be met through your own relationship with God.

Do you believe you and your fiancé share the same spiritual convictions?

Obviously we all are on a journey, and no one is perfect, but who would you say puts more energy into their spiritual life? You? Your fiancé? How does that make you feel?

Currently, what role does God play in your relationship as a couple?

Read the following statements and check the boxes that most closely align with your feelings. Discuss your answers with each other and your premarital counselor or mentor.

Church attendance is important.

O yes   O no   O undecided   Potential Action _____

I would like praying together to be part of our relationship.

O yes   O no   O undecided   Potential Action _____

I am committed to investing time in the service of others.

O yes   O no   O undecided   Potential Action _____

I feel comfortable discussing spiritual issues with my fiancé.

O yes   O no   O undecided   Potential Action _____

I would like to develop a regular time of personal Bible study and prayer.

O yes   O no   O undecided   Potential Action _____

It would be a real boost to our relationship to find a marriage mentor couple who could guide us in the spiritual dimension of our life.

O yes   O no   O undecided   Potential Action _____

As you discuss the spiritual dimensions of your relationship, it's important to realize that how you experience and express faith can be influenced by your history, personality, and values. Your faith journey doesn't have to look exactly like your fiancé's. Instead of looking for sameness, look for significant places of overlap in how you express your faith as well as similar levels of commitment. Find the places you can come together spiritually, and accept the places where each person's journey with God is unique.

In her book *The Good News About Marriage*, Shaunti Feldhahn claims that couples who have an active faith actually lower their chance of divorce:

> The rate of divorce in the church is 25 to 50 percent lower than among those who don't attend worship services, and those who prioritize their faith and/ or pray together are dramatically happier and more connected.[1]

Couples who have a similar faith background and integrate their faith into their relationship have less marital conflict. We want this for you, and we hope you'll consider starting now! We confidently believe that the best way to develop spiritual intimacy and compatibility in your marriage is to begin growing together spiritually prior to your wedding day.

When we're together (or with our premarital counselor), be sure to talk about:

Date we discussed this exercise:

2

EXERCISE TWO

Committing to the "Closer Challenge"

Marriage experts point out that couples who are spiritually connected have greater satisfaction in their marriage and physical intimacy, and do a more effective job of raising their children.

Because of this reality, we've created the "Closer Challenge," a twenty-minute commitment one day per week. It's a clear, concise challenge that is very doable for couples to invest in one another spiritually. To accept this challenge, you both need to be able to say yes to these two questions:

> " The divorce rate in America is horrible. However, studies show that if a couple prays together on a daily basis, there is about a one in one thousand chance of them getting a divorce. As marriage therapists, my colleagues and I would be out of jobs if couples just prayed together on a regular basis.[2]

1. Are you willing to pray together on a regular basis?

If it's too uncomfortable to pray aloud, you can simply hold hands and pray silently together. Prayer is merely setting aside intentional time to talk to or be with God. As a couple, when you pray together, you are acknowledging that you want God to play the primary role in your hearts as individuals and in your relationship.

- ○ Yes, I am willing to pray with my spouse on a regular basis.

> " Many couples are simply too busy or distracted and haven't committed to making spiritual growth a priority.

2. Are you willing to spend twenty minutes together each week to engage in faith conversations?

When we're together (or with our premarital counselor), be sure to talk about:

Twenty minutes doesn't seem like a lot of time, but unless there is a strong commitment to come together for this "spiritual intimacy appointment," those few minutes won't even happen. This is an entry-level time commitment; it can increase as you feel more natural and comfortable. Your time together can take any form that works for you: reading selected scriptures, reading from a couples' devotional book, or simply discussing what God is teaching you through your own spiritual journey.

○ Yes, I will commit to investing twenty minutes of disciplined time together to work on spiritual intimacy each week.

"

Jim and Cathy Burns wrote an excellent couple's devotional called *Closer: 52 Devotions to Draw Couples Together*. It includes fifty-two short devotions and questions that fit perfectly with the Closer Challenge. You can find this and more marriage resources at www.homeword.com.

If you and/or your fiancé can't make these commitments right now, what type of spiritual commitment can you make that will enhance your faith as a couple?

Date we discussed this exercise:

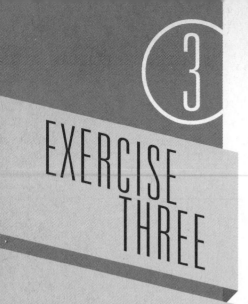

EXERCISE THREE

Finding a Marriage Mentor Couple

One of the best ways to increase your spiritual intimacy as a couple is to find a mentor couple who can help guide you to deeper and more meaningful places in your faith and marriage.

The first few years of your marriage are critical to ensure its success. Let us assure you that you don't have to journey alone! Many wonderful couples are willing to come alongside you—**you just need to ask.**

Look for a couple who is older, wiser, and more experienced, who will be safe for you to share your joys and struggles with. The time with these mentors can be as formal as working through this workbook with you or as informal as a meeting every few months where you ask them specific questions about faith and marriage. Try to find this couple before your wedding day so you're receiving wise input prior to getting married.

List three couples who could become potential marriage mentors:

What do you hope to get out of the time you spend with a marriage mentor couple?

How will you ask them? Think through exactly what you will say. If couples have never been mentors before, they may not know what you're expecting, so be clear. Most couples will be honored that you asked them. If the first meeting goes well, ask for an opportunity to meet again.

> **Keep in mind that marriage mentors are not necessarily trained counselors, but they are gracious people who are supportive, encouraging, and can offer practical input as they share their lives with you.**

Pray for God to guide you to the right couple.

After a time of prayer, call one of the couples from your list and set a date for your first meeting.

After you've logged some of your own years of being married, be sure to become mentors to a younger couple. Pay it back! Take notes on what you're learning now, because chances are good you'll be able to use them someday.

When we're together (or with our premarital counselor), be sure to talk about:

Date we discussed this exercise:

CHAPTER NINE

REMARRIAGE: A FRESH START

Some of the finest couples we encounter are those who have experienced deep pain or loss in a previous marriage and then remarried. There is great hope and joy to be found in remarriage!

Some remarriages are a result of divorce, while others occur after the death of a spouse. Regardless of your situation, remarriage is often more complicated than a first marriage and requires a lot of additional work. These exercises will help you learn from your past—one that usually involves pain—to prepare for your future in a most wonderful way.

Exercises

☐ What I Have Learned from My Past

☐ Successfully Blending a Family

☐ Remarriage Readiness Survey

EXERCISE ONE

What I Have Learned from My Past

One of the primary reasons a remarriage fails is because the husband or wife (or both) didn't learn from their past relationship. If you are unwilling to do the work of looking back, then often you are unwilling to work on this next marriage as well. However, if you take the time and are disciplined enough to learn from your past, you won't repeat the same mistakes in the future.

Be Brutally Honest about Your Own Brokenness

What areas of brokenness did you bring to your previous marriage?

What issues do you take responsibility for in your divorce?

> Our experience with remarriages is that the strongest ones don't emerge on the rebound from the first. Health appears only after both people have completely dealt with their past.

What mistakes did you make that caused tension, lack of intimacy, or miscommunication?

What could you have done differently that you plan to change in your new relationship?

Make Peace with Your Past

Have you made peace with your past relationship? If it was a divorce, what resentment or bitterness do you still carry?

If your ex-spouse came back to you and asked if you would be willing to give it another try, what would you tell him or her?

Do you have any unfinished business with your past marriage? Anything that needs to be addressed with other relationships, such as ex in-laws or neighbors, from that season of your life? If so, what actions should you take?

If you are a parent, what can you learn from your past parenting experiences that you will bring to this new relationship?

> The ghost of marriages past can become very present in your new relationship if you're not careful. Being aware of this reality can save you from surprise pain. Someone once said, "The past has very little substance, but it stays close to your heels."[1]

Move Forward with Confidence

Give three reasons why you're sure this relationship will be a success.

Do you feel confident that you have done the work necessary to make this relationship succeed? If so, what have you done? If not, what's still needed?

Have you moved forward with all the financial, legal, and child issues that you need to in order to begin a healthy remarriage?

Do you believe you have had the proper premarital preparation for your new marriage? What are the issues that still need to be worked through?

When we're together (or with our premarital counselor), be sure to talk about:

In some relationships, it's only one person who has been previously married. If that is the case for you, what do you see as potential hurdles?

Date we discussed this exercise:

EXERCISE TWO

Successfully Blending a Family

Many remarriages have the added issues of stepparenting and blending families. If remarriages with children aren't handled well, a barrier to marriage oneness can quickly develop, resulting in diminished intimacy. When you combine a remarriage with kids, stepparenting, ex-wives, ex-husbands, in-laws, holidays, different parenting styles, and diverse lifestyles, the potential for tension is much greater.

This exercise represents the two major issues of stepparenting and blended-family topics that need to be thoroughly discussed before marriage.

> This is not always the case, but many couples say that managing their own relationship as a couple is easy compared to the challenge of dealing with the children in their new relationship.

The Children

DISCIPLINE: What will our approach be?

○ Yes, we've talked   ○ Need to talk more
○ Haven't started this discussion yet

FINANCES: Who pays for what?

○ Yes, we've talked   ○ Need to talk more
○ Haven't started this discussion yet

SCHOOL: How will we handle education issues?

○ Yes, we've talked   ○ Need to talk more
○ Haven't started this discussion yet

LIVING SITUATION: Will the children be going back and forth between homes?

○ Yes, we've talked   ○ Need to talk more
○ Haven't started this discussion yet

HOLIDAYS: What is the plan and what understandings have been reached with ex-spouses if they are involved?

○ Yes, we've talked   ○ Need to talk more
○ Haven't started this discussion yet

> Stepfamilies that are flexible, sacrificial, creative, and take extra time to plan are the ones that see the most reward for their efforts.

Ex-Spouses

BOUNDARIES: Is there clear communication about what is acceptable with the ex?

○ Yes, we've talked   ○ Need to talk more
○ Haven't started this discussion yet

COMMUNICATION: How often will we talk with the ex?

○ Yes, we've talked   ○ Need to talk more
○ Haven't started this discussion yet

FINANCES: Is it clear how much money is needed to support the kids?

○ Yes, we've talked   ○ Need to talk more
○ Haven't started this discussion yet

LEGAL: Are there any pending issues that could require legality?

○ Yes, we've talked   ○ Need to talk more
○ Haven't started this discussion yet

GRANDPARENTS: Will we still be involved in their lives?

○ Yes, we've talked   ○ Need to talk more
○ Haven't started this discussion yet

HONOR WITH INTEGRITY: How will we speak about or treat the ex?

○ Yes, we've talked   ○ Need to talk more
○ Haven't started this discussion yet

When we're together (or with our premarital counselor), be sure to talk about:

Date we discussed this exercise:

EXERCISE THREE

Remarriage Readiness Survey

This remarriage readiness survey will help you see if there are still issues you need to deal with personally or as a couple. We highly encourage you to work through the previous two exercises in this chapter prior to completing the survey.

First, answer these questions about yourself and your own level of readiness. Then, after you've taken the survey, rate where you think your fiancé is on the scale.

> Divorce is a huge loss! It's a loss of home, often a loss of finances, and definitely a loss of the way things were. Divorce also involves more than just you.

1. I believe I have learned all I can from my past marriage and made the appropriate adjustments and changes.

	Not at All				So-So				Absolutely	
Me:	1	2	3	4	5	6	7	8	9	10
Fiancé:	1	2	3	4	5	6	7	8	9	10

2. I am coming into this marriage with appropriate expectations.

	Not at All				So-So				Absolutely	
Me:	1	2	3	4	5	6	7	8	9	10
Fiancé:	1	2	3	4	5	6	7	8	9	10

3. I have dealt with all that I can from my past.

	Not at All				So-So				Absolutely	
Me:	1	2	3	4	5	6	7	8	9	10
Fiancé:	1	2	3	4	5	6	7	8	9	10

4. [If there are children] My fiancé and I are on the same page about stepchildren and parenting issues.

	Not at All				So-So				Absolutely	
Me:	1	2	3	4	5	6	7	8	9	10
Fiancé:	1	2	3	4	5	6	7	8	9	10

5. I have not kept secrets from my fiancé.

	Not at All				So-So				Absolutely	
Me:	1	2	3	4	5	6	7	8	9	10
Fiancé:	1	2	3	4	5	6	7	8	9	10

6. I have lived my physical relationship with my fiancé with integrity and honor.

	Not at All				So-So				Absolutely	
Me:	1	2	3	4	5	6	7	8	9	10
Fiancé:	1	2	3	4	5	6	7	8	9	10

7. I have discussed all financial issues and responsibilities with my fiancé.

	Not at All			So-So					Absolutely
Me:	1	2	3	4	5	6	7	8	9	10
Fiancé:	1	2	3	4	5	6	7	8	9	10

8. I have talked to my extended community and invited them to give me input into our relationship.

	Not at All			So-So					Absolutely
Me:	1	2	3	4	5	6	7	8	9	10
Fiancé:	1	2	3	4	5	6	7	8	9	10

9. There are no red flags in our relationship that I have not either dealt with or am dealing with in a healthy way.

	Not at All			So-So					Absolutely
Me:	1	2	3	4	5	6	7	8	9	10
Fiancé:	1	2	3	4	5	6	7	8	9	10

10. I understand the communication and conflict issues of our relationship and believe I have the tools to thrive.

	Not at All			So-So					Absolutely
Me:	1	2	3	4	5	6	7	8	9	10
Fiancé:	1	2	3	4	5	6	7	8	9	10

11. I believe I am ready for remarriage.

	Not at All			So-So					Absolutely
Me:	1	2	3	4	5	6	7	8	9	10
Fiancé:	1	2	3	4	5	6	7	8	9	10

" In all remarriage situations, we strongly urge you to go to GettingReadyForMarriage.com and work through the online tool.

When we're together (or with our premarital counselor), be sure to talk about:

Date we discussed this exercise:

123

A Message to Pastors, Counselors, and Marriage Mentors

Thank you for caring so much about helping couples build strong marriages from the ground up. We applaud you for investing your time and energy in the service of others.

We also want to thank you for choosing to use this material as part of your premarital counseling. Of course, you may choose to use this resource however works best for you, but we have several suggestions for how to make the most of it.

1. Encourage the couple to read our book *Getting Ready for Marriage*. While it is highly suggested, it's not mandatory that they read the book in order to complete the exercises in this workbook. The exercises will stand on their own without the contents from the book; however, reading the book will provide more details and context on each topic, equipping the couple to be better informed as they go through the exercises.

2. Each person should have his or her own workbook. This allows the individual time to reflect on the exercises in private and feel safe enough to write down his or her feelings. Our experience has been that couples are more honest when reflecting and writing in their own workbook than when they share writing space. Please encourage them to go this route.

3. Couples will benefit most from the *Getting Ready for Marriage Workbook* by completing every exercise. If they do one exercise per week, they will finish the book in roughly nine months. They could also pick up the pace and do one chapter per week (or every two weeks) as opposed to one exercise. We realize that everyone's time frame for their premarital counseling is unique, and so we encourage you to talk about timing during your initial meeting with the couple. Agree to a schedule that works for you and for the couple. If there simply isn't enough time to complete the entire workbook prior to the wedding, discuss which exercises you think will be most valuable with the couple you're mentoring and ask them to work on those specific ones.

4. We have created an incredible online tool to enhance a couple's premarital education experience that will make your job easier. This tool includes six short video teaching segments, humor vignettes, and communication exercises. When the couple completes all sessions, they will receive a certificate. By encouraging couples to pursue the certificate, you can be assured that they've received some solid premarital instruction. You can learn more about how you can use this online tool at www.GettingReadyForMarriage.com.

If you are new to couples mentoring, here are a few tips:

1. *Don't talk too much.* The goal of a marriage mentor or counselor is to facilitate good discussion about important issues.

2. *Take notice of sensitive topics and push for clarity.* Gently encourage couples to ask further questions and dive deeper into more sensitive issues. With you present, it may be easier for them to honestly share than when they are on their own. When you notice something that needs further discussion, point it out. You're more than a friend—you're guiding them toward a healthier marriage, and sometimes, that route may pass through difficulty.

3. *Do talk a little.* Feel free to share appropriate stories from your own experience. You don't need to feel pressure to have a perfect marriage; openly tell them lessons you've learned from your own decisions—good or bad. Most helpful lessons are conceived through difficulty. Don't dominate the session, but do illuminate when it will be helpful.

4. *Don't be afraid to bring up red flags you see in the relationship.* If you have concerns, gently bring them up. You may be the only person who cares enough to confront the couple in a healthy manner. Also, if the red flags are a deep concern and you are not a licensed marriage counselor, refer them to someone who can address deeper, core issues.

5. *Offer care and mentoring after the wedding.* If you are willing and have time, we find that some of the best and most helpful conversations happen *after* the wedding. As we wrote in our book *Getting Ready for Marriage*, engaged couples aren't always willing to look at the more significant issues during engagement, and so they will need someone to go to after marriage.

Congratulations!

1. Sharon Jayson, "Premarital Education Could Cut Divorce Rate," June 22, 2006, *USA Today*, http://usatoday30.usatoday.com/news/education/2006-06-21-premarital-education_x.htm?csp=34.

Chapter 2—Writing Your Marriage Script Through Goals, Hopes, and Expectations

1. Drs. Les Parrott and Leslie Parrott, *Saving Your Marriage Before It Starts: Seven Questions to Ask Before—and After—You Marry* (Grand Rapids, MI: Zondervan, 2006), 15.

2. Ray Johnston, *The Hope Quotient: Measure It. Raise It. You'll Never Be the Same* (Nashville, TN: Thomas Nelson, 2014), 13.

3. Edwin Louis Cole, BrainyQuote, www.brainyquote.com/quotes/e/edwinlouis170162.html.

Chapter 4—Communication: The Fastest Route to Connection

1. Drs. Les Parrott and Leslie Parrott, *Saving Your Marriage Before It Starts: Seven Questions to Ask Before—and After—You Marry* (Grand Rapids, MI: Zondervan, 2006), 79.

Chapter 6—Finances: The Best Things in Life Are Not Things

1. Dave Ramsey, *Total Money Makeover: A Proven Plan for Financial Fitness* (Nashville, TN: Thomas Nelson, 2013), 104–13.

Chapter 7—Sexuality: The Naked Truth

1. "Top 10 Reasons Marriages Fail," Divorce.com, http://divorce.com/top-10-reasons-marriages-fail.

2. Gary and Barbara Rosberg, *The 5 Sex Needs of Men and Women: Discover the Secrets of Great Sex in a Godly Marriage* (Carol Stream, IL: Tyndale, 2007), 40.

Chapter 8—Spiritual Intimacy: The Power of Compatibility

1. Shaunti Feldhahn, *The Good News About Marriage: Debunking Discouraging Myths About Marriage and Divorce* (Colorado Springs, CO: WaterBrook Multnomah, 2014), 86.

2. Dr. Dave Stoop in Jim Burns and Doug Fields, *Getting Ready for Marriage: A Practical Road Map for Your Journey Together* (Colorado Springs, CO: David C Cook, 2014), 164.

Chapter 9—Remarriage: A Fresh Start

1. Jim Burns and Doug Fields, *Getting Ready for Marriage: A Practical Road Map for Your Journey Together* (Colorado Springs, CO: David C Cook, 2014), 177.

ACKNOWLEDGMENTS

So many people influenced this *Getting Ready for Marriage* project and helped make it possible. We are deeply grateful to them.

To Heather McGrath and the Legacy Foundation for your generosity and vision to help us create the incredible online communication tools for GettingReadyforMarriage.com.

To Helen Lovaas and the God's Charitable Gift Foundation for helping fund this workbook. While writing this workbook, Helen entered into eternity. Her legacy will go on for generations to come. We at HomeWord are deeply indebted to Helen and her husband, Lee, for investing and believing in us.

To the Wheeler Family Charitable Trust for stepping up to help us create some amazing videos for our online communication tool for engaged couples. Thank you so much for your years of support.

To Steve and Sue Perry and the Sacred Harvest Foundation, who challenged us to create the "Refreshing Your Marriage" content and conference. Much of this material came from your prodding to change the way we look at marriage education.

To Cindy Ward for once again going way beyond the call of duty. We are so grateful for all your effort and talent.

To Jim Liebelt for being one of the most remarkable people we know. We are so grateful for the many ways you make our lives better. Your incredibly valuable insight, research, and can-do attitude make you the MVP of any of our projects.

To Kevin and Lindsey Cram, Kyle and Kylee Cleveland, Chris Reed, Matt McGill, and Rendi Miller for reading this manuscript and helping make it better. We deeply thank you. We spent a day looking over all your insight and ideas and said yes to almost all your thoughts. Your combined efforts made this a much better product, and we are grateful.

To Andrew Accardy and Seth Bartlette for your creativity, leadership, and brilliance. We know this entire project is better because of you both. We wanted to change the way premarital education is done, and we think with this project we reached that goal because of you. We are so grateful.

We are also deeply grateful to our wives, Cathy and Cathy, and our children for "being there" for us during this project. Part of our passion for doing the *Getting Ready for Marriage* project was to help our own children make great decisions about marriage.